ACHIEVING WORK-LIFE BALANCE

ACHIEVING WORK-LIFE BALANCE

ZARIA DUSK

CONTENTS

Introduction to Work-Life Balance   1

1 Understanding the Impact of Imbalance   4

2 Strategies for Balancing Work and Life   7

3 Building a Support System   11

4 Self-Care Practices   14

5 Technology and Work-Life Balance   18

6 Cultural and Organizational Factors   21

7 Work-Life Balance in Different Professions   24

8 Maintaining Balance Over Time   27

Conclusion and Future Trends   30

Copyright © 2025 by Zaria Dusk
All rights reserved. No part of this book may be reproduced in any manner whatsoever without written permission except in the case of brief quotations embodied in critical articles and reviews.
First Printing, 2025

Introduction to Work-Life Balance

Work-life balance refers to the ability of an individual to maintain a healthy separation between personal life and professional responsibilities. This equilibrium has become one of the most sought-after job characteristics, as employees increasingly prioritize a harmonious relationship between their work and personal lives. However, achieving this balance is more challenging today than ever before. Modern technology keeps employees tethered to their workplaces, even during personal time, creating blurred boundaries.

The United States holds the distinction of being one of the most overworked nations globally. Research reveals that Americans often place greater value on work than on personal and leisure activities. Unfortunately, the significance of work-life balance is often fully recognized only after a crisis occurs—whether it's health-related burnout, strained personal relationships, or job turnover. Among job-seekers, particularly skilled women, the ability to maintain work-life balance is a crucial factor when evaluating employment opportunities.

Work-life balance is also a source of tension within organizations. There is an ongoing conflict between employees' desire for more family or personal time and businesses' demands for extended working hours to maximize productivity. This persistent struggle directly impacts job satisfaction, which, in turn, influences overall happiness and life satisfaction.

Defining Work-Life Balance

It's important to recognize that work-life balance means different things to different people. Individuals' perspectives on balance are shaped by their unique experiences, personality traits, and specific needs. Moreover, definitions of work-life balance vary, ranging from conceptual to practical interpretations. The way balance is experienced also depends on the social and cultural contexts of a particular setting.

In essence, work-life balance can be understood as a state where no single domain—be it work or personal life—overshadows the other. While this discussion highlights the experiences of full-time office administrators in Johannesburg, South Africa, the insights and strategies explored here are universally applicable to any workplace or profession across the globe.

The modern workplace has amplified the relevance of work-life balance. Factors such as technological advancements, globalization, fluid job roles, and the rise of contract-based employment have made crossing the boundaries of work and personal life a daily reality for many. Despite the general consensus that work and personal life can coexist, this ideal often eludes organizations and society at large. When employees perceive a lack of balance, it inevitably leads to organizational inefficiencies and performance challenges.

The Importance and Benefits of Work-Life Balance

Work-life balance is vital for individuals at all stages of life. Demographic, economic, and social changes have made it increasingly difficult for people to juggle work with family life, hobbies, and other personal pursuits. This imbalance often results in skill shortages and decreased job satisfaction, underscoring the critical need for balanced living.

When achieved, work-life balance offers numerous benefits. It empowers employees with a sense of control over when, where, and how they work. This balance is not just a personal victory—it represents a shared benefit for individuals, businesses, and society as a whole. For example, many European employees work fewer than 60 hours per week, devoting a significant portion of their days to family, leisure, and personal growth. This approach promotes health, well-being, and a renewed sense of purpose in both personal and professional spheres.

Flexible work arrangements are another cornerstone of successful work-life balance initiatives. Flexibility enables individuals to integrate their work responsibilities with personal commitments seamlessly. When organizations respect employees' rights to a fulfilling life inside and outside of work, they foster a culture of mutual respect and collaboration that benefits everyone.

CHAPTER 1

Understanding the Impact of Imbalance

Periods of imbalance are inevitable for everyone. When we feel overwhelmed, our responses may vary: some of us may immerse ourselves in work to escape the feeling, while others seek comfort in spending more time with family and friends, pursuing hobbies, or engaging in recreational activities. Some may attempt to restore balance through altered eating or sleeping habits. However, the effects of imbalance often manifest through symptoms such as fatigue, boredom, worry, discontent, impaired concentration, or even physical exhaustion. These signals indicate the need for a "release valve" in our system—a necessary slack that prevents overload. When personal or work time dominates disproportionately, the consequences extend beyond diminished productivity, impacting overall health and well-being. This underscores the importance of continually reflecting on and striving for work-life balance.

Though everyone's definition of success varies, many individuals share a common desire: to enjoy both professional satisfaction and personal fulfillment. Yet, in the relentless pace of today's world, achieving a perfect 50-50 equilibrium seems increasingly elusive. Demanding work schedules, such as MBA boot camps, night shifts, and round-the-clock connectivity via smartphones, have blurred the line between work and personal time. The results are striking—rising stress levels, deteriorating physical and mental health, and strained family relationships are just a few consequences.

Health Consequences

Imbalances between work and personal life can significantly impact physical and mental health. Data from the U.S. Census Bureau highlights that employed individuals over the age of 25 who have never married—and do not have children under 18—work an average of 39.7 hours per week. This is slightly lower than the 43-hour average seen in older demographic groups, yet the effects of work pressure remain palpable.

For single parents, the burden is even more pronounced, with employment often linked to higher rates of illness, increased medical care usage, and reliance on public health assistance. High-pressure jobs have been shown to negatively affect cardiovascular health, including reduced left ventricular ejection fraction—a measure of the heart's pumping efficiency. Meanwhile, part-time workers with inconsistent schedules are at a heightened risk for adverse health outcomes, largely due to increased household responsibilities and diminished personal time. This situation underscores the inadequacy of simplistic measures, like average work hours, in accurately reflecting work-life conflict and its health implications.

Research in fields such as health economics, organizational studies, and public policy continues to unravel the relationship between work schedules, stress, health outcomes, and work-life balance. The evidence consistently points to the need for a deliberate, balanced approach to mitigate severe physical and mental health consequences.

Relationship Strain

The effects of overwork extend beyond physical health—they strain relationships as well. According to the American Psychological Association (APA), 42% of adults feel workplace expectations leave them overly busy. For parents, the impact is even more pronounced, with four in ten workers reporting increased tensions at home due to work-related stress.

Job stress not only affects interactions between employees and their families but also shapes broader family dynamics. Parents struggling to balance work and child-rearing responsibilities may feel unsupported by rigid workplace policies. Commuting distances, inflexible hours, and unsympathetic employers exacerbate this strain. On the other hand, organizations with family-friendly initiatives—such as flexible scheduling, parental leave, and teamwork-based approaches—help foster better work-life integration. Such policies benefit not only employees but also their families and partnerships.

Busy careers often pose challenges to personal relationships, particularly for women. Professional women are frequently criticized unfairly for pursuing ambitious careers while navigating traditional expectations of marriage and motherhood. Social perceptions often perpetuate the belief that thriving careers are inherently incompatible with fertility, successful parenting, or fulfilling romantic relationships. These stereotypes can create obstacles for both conventional and non-traditional families. Forward-thinking organizations that prioritize harmonious work-life policies are increasingly valued, especially by women seeking to balance their personal and professional aspirations.

CHAPTER 2

Strategies for Balancing Work and Life

Finding harmony between work and personal life is a continuous process that requires intentional planning, flexibility, and self-awareness. Below are six strategies to help you implement and maintain a sustainable work-life balance:

1. **Set SMART Goals** The foundation of work-life balance lies in goal-setting. Use the SMART framework to set goals that are specific, measurable, attainable, relevant, and time-bound. For instance, set a goal to take a vacation within the next 12 months or commit to leaving work by a specific time daily. These goals provide direction and help you prioritize, enabling you to allocate time effectively between work and personal activities.
2. **Plan Effectively** Time management starts with strategic planning. Use a planner or calendar to schedule both work-related and personal activities. By managing your time in advance, you can avoid overcommitting and ensure that you have space for relaxation and hobbies. Effective planning also

helps you maintain a holistic view of your responsibilities, preventing them from becoming overwhelming.
3. **Make the Most of Your Time** Perfectionism can drain both time and energy. Instead of aiming to be an overachiever, focus on completing tasks efficiently and use the time saved for personal enrichment. After finishing your workday, commit to disconnecting and focusing on activities or people that matter to you. Establishing clear distinctions between work time and personal time fosters a healthier routine for both.
4. **Prioritize Self-Care** Your health is the foundation of all productivity. Without proper self-care, it becomes difficult to care for others or perform at your best. Make sleep, healthy eating, and regular exercise non-negotiable priorities. Practices like meditation, yoga, or simply unwinding with a good book can go a long way in managing daily stress. Treat self-care not as a luxury, but as an essential part of maintaining equilibrium.
5. **Communicate and Establish Boundaries** Open communication is essential for balancing work and personal life. Discuss your work-life needs with your employer, colleagues, and family members to set clear, mutually respectful boundaries. For instance, inform your supervisor of any personal interruptions that may occur during remote work, such as family-related situations. Ensure these boundaries are reinforced with consistent communication so that both parties uphold them.
6. **Set a Schedule and Stick to It** Routine is the key to achieving long-term work-life balance. Determine work hours that align with your energy levels and responsibilities. For example, you might find morning work more productive due to fewer meetings or prefer an afternoon schedule that allows you to start the day with a mental reset. Incorporate breaks, meal

times, and personal activities into your schedule. A well-structured routine not only enhances focus but also reduces the chances of burnout.

Time Management Techniques

Mastering time management is integral to achieving work-life balance. Here are some practical tips to optimize your time effectively:

- **Set Daily Goals:** Each day is unique. Plan your priorities and ensure that you're focusing on tasks that align with your larger goals. Break your day into manageable blocks to stay organized and productive.
- **Eliminate Non-Essential Activities:** Avoid spending time on tasks that add little value. Delegate or minimize activities that do not align with your priorities.
- **Avoid Multitasking:** Focus on completing one task at a time for better efficiency and quality. Dedicate specific time blocks to each activity, followed by short breaks to recharge.
- **Incorporate "Me Time":** Dedicate time daily for relaxation or personal hobbies. This helps maintain your mental and emotional health, making you more energized for work and other commitments.

Setting Boundaries

Creating boundaries is crucial for maintaining control over your life and well-being, especially when working remotely. Here are actionable strategies for setting boundaries:

- **Define Work Hours:** Work with your employer to create a schedule that aligns with your needs. Stick to this routine con-

sistently, ensuring you take breaks and maintain an end time for your workday. This helps prevent overworking and allows for better rest and recovery.
- **Prioritize Personal Time:** Schedule moments for family, friends, and personal growth. Whether it's a lunch break, a walk, or time spent on a hobby, these activities recharge your mind and foster connections.
- **Communicate Expectations:** Clearly outline your availability and limitations with colleagues, supervisors, and even family members. This proactive approach ensures that work demands and personal needs do not conflict unnecessarily.
- **Follow Healthy Habits:** Avoid skipping meals or neglecting exercise. Eating well and staying active are essential for maintaining long-term balance and resilience.

CHAPTER 3

Building a Support System

Creating a reliable support system is fundamental to achieving a balanced and fulfilling life. A strong network of family, friends, mentors, and colleagues can provide encouragement, guidance, and resources when you need them the most. Here's a closer look at how these relationships can help you thrive.

Communicating Fairness in Relationships In relationships, particularly marriage, open discussions about fairness and shared responsibilities are essential. Partners must collaboratively define what "fair" means, ensuring that both parties feel valued and supported. If you and your partner plan to have children, your careers should collectively enable you to manage childcare effectively—whether that involves utilizing full-time daycare or adjusting work hours during your children's early years. Certain career paths may naturally accommodate this balance better than others. Having these conversations early allows you to plan proactively and avoid potential conflicts later.

For working women, the need for support extends beyond personal relationships to professional settings. Careers often demand relentless focus, and the pressure to excel can feel overwhelming.

From my experience, you can't do it all on your own. Seeking advice from others who have navigated similar paths is invaluable. I recall my fellow residents emphasizing the challenges of transitioning to a leadership role during the third year of residency—it was a critical period of learning, growth, and building a foundation for long-term success.

Building a support system often takes years, but it pays dividends over time. Peers, mentors, and colleagues provide wisdom that can help you tackle obstacles more efficiently. Great advice from those who have walked similar paths can save months—or even years—on the learning curve.

Family and Friends Achieving balance affects not only you but also the people closest to you—your partner, parents, children, and friends. A lack of balance can create tension in these relationships, leading to misunderstandings and conflict. Prioritizing the people who bring joy and meaning to your life is essential. Together, you and your loved ones can harness each other's strengths to enhance both your career and personal fulfillment.

Your closest relationships play a vital role in maintaining your emotional well-being. Friends allow you to escape work-related stress and offer a fresh perspective, while family members bring unparalleled understanding and support. They can act as your foundation, offering stability and motivation during challenging times.

Even in the workplace, having strong relationships can help you stay grounded. Workmates who support and collaborate with you form a crucial network to reduce stress and foster a positive environment. Good relationships—whether personal or professional—help you remain relaxed, balanced, and happy in various situations.

Mentors and Coaches A mentor can be transformative in your journey toward work-life balance and personal growth. This person might be a more experienced colleague, a family member, or someone who has achieved success in an area you aspire to excel in. The role of a mentor is not to push you into competition but to guide you toward discovering your potential. Through their wisdom and insights, mentors encourage you to step out of your comfort zone, take risks, and learn from experiences.

Mentorship is a process of growth, allowing you to see truths in your own way. Great mentors provide guidance without imposing their own agenda, helping you succeed on your terms. Similarly, a coach offers focused support to help you achieve specific goals, whether personal or professional. Coaches and mentors serve as trusted advisors, offering clarity during turbulent times and empowering you to navigate challenges with confidence.

The truth is that no one achieves work-life success alone. Building a network of mentors and seeking regular guidance ensures continuous growth. Whether it's through shared experiences, constructive feedback, or a fresh perspective, these relationships help you grow into the person you're meant to be.

Conclusion A robust support system—built on the pillars of family, friends, mentors, and colleagues—can dramatically improve your ability to navigate the complexities of work and life. By leaning on these relationships for guidance and encouragement, you can foster balance, resilience, and success in all areas of your life.

CHAPTER 4

Self-Care Practices

Self-care is an essential component of maintaining overall well-being, especially in today's fast-paced and demanding world. By intentionally carving out moments for self-care, we can recharge our mental, emotional, and physical energy. Below are practical approaches to self-care, categorized for ease of implementation:

1. Sensory Self-Care Tap into the healing power of your five senses to create moments of soothing comfort. These practices include:

- Embracing a hug or other loving touch to foster a sense of connection and warmth.
- Inhaling calming aromas—try essential oils or a favorite scent to relax your mind.
- Lighting a candle and watching the flame flicker, creating a moment of stillness.
- Listening to gentle, soothing sounds, such as soft music, nature recordings, or guided meditations.
- Wrapping yourself in a warm blanket to feel safe and nurtured.

2. Hydrating Self-Care Never underestimate the power of hydration. Close your eyes and sip a refreshing drink, allowing the sensation to revitalize and nourish your body. Reflect on how such a simple practice sustains and energizes you—hydration is a cornerstone of physical wellness.

3. Nourishing Self-Care Fuel your body with wholesome, satisfying meals that provide lasting energy. Choose nutrient-rich foods that "stick to your ribs," giving you the strength to carry on and face daily challenges.

4. Energizing Self-Care Incorporate physical activities that uplift your spirit and energize your body. Whether it's a brisk walk up and down the stairs, a quick yoga session, or dancing to a favorite song, these moments of movement can reinvigorate you, both physically and mentally.

Commit to Self-Care Creating time for self-care—even just 5–10 minutes a day—can make an enormous difference. Proceed with a spirit of gentleness, curiosity, and adaptability. Explore practices that resonate with you, adjust those that don't, and maintain a mindset of self-compassion. Remember, even the busiest schedule has room for these moments of rejuvenation.

Physical Well-Being Physical health often takes a back seat during busy periods, but neglecting it can lead to significant consequences—poorer health, lower productivity, and heightened stress. To maintain physical well-being, consider these practices:

- Prioritize 7–8 hours of sleep each night. Quality rest is critical for restoration and focus.
- Begin your day with a nutritious, energizing breakfast to fuel your body.
- Incorporate regular exercise, especially in the morning when energy levels may be highest.

- Schedule and take lunch breaks to recharge during your workday.
- End office work at a timely hour to prevent burnout and allow for relaxation.

Stress often leads to irregular eating patterns and comfort-food binges, which can disrupt sleep. Drinking water consistently can reduce sugar cravings and maintain energy throughout the day. Ultimately, treating your body with care helps reduce stress and promotes better concentration, productivity, and overall quality of life.

Mental Health Mental well-being is just as important as physical health in achieving work-life balance. Employees often juggle personal and professional responsibilities, making it vital to approach work with a peaceful and organized mind. A supportive work environment can significantly impact mental health, reducing stress and fostering happiness.

Twenty years ago, burnout was first identified as a syndrome of emotional exhaustion, detachment, and diminished personal accomplishment. This condition, often triggered by prolonged physical or psychological stress, has only become more prevalent in today's demanding work culture. Stress in the workplace not only affects mental health but also influences perceptions of security and safety, key values for an individual's sense of well-being.

To promote mental health, workplaces should prioritize job control and decision-making latitude, allowing employees to navigate their responsibilities with autonomy. Family-friendly policies, reasonable work hours, fair wages, and health protections are essential to fostering a culture of balance and safety. By advocating for these measures, organizations can create healthier, more supportive environments for their employees.

Conclusion Self-care, physical well-being, and mental health are interconnected pillars of a balanced life. When you prioritize these aspects, you build a foundation for sustained happiness, productivity, and success—both personally and professionally.

CHAPTER 5

Technology and Work-Life Balance

Technology itself is neither inherently "good" nor "bad." It holds immense potential to enhance our lives, especially in bridging the gap between professional and personal domains. Innovations like Information Communication Technology (ICT) have revolutionized flexible working arrangements, allowing individuals to work from home or remote locations. Smart technology, when thoughtfully integrated into work-life balance programs, can empower employees to meet both their professional and personal commitments with greater ease.

However, challenges arise when technology is mismanaged. The same tools that facilitate flexibility can also blur boundaries between work and personal life, leading to work intensification. For instance, the constant connectivity enabled by smartphones, laptops, and the internet can tempt individuals to remain perpetually accessible, even during personal time. Those who struggle to establish clear boundaries may find themselves consumed by work, using it as a way to avoid personal or relationship issues. This "always-on" culture makes it crucial to set firm boundaries around technology use to protect work-life balance.

Digital Detox

Taking a break from the digital world can work wonders for your mental health and overall well-being. Engaging in a digital detox offers numerous benefits: improved mental clarity, deeper connections with loved ones, enhanced presence in the moment, better sleep quality, more free time, and sharper focus on tasks at hand.

If you're feeling tethered to your devices, consider an experiment: turn off all sound and visual notifications on your phone for a day. You'll discover that the world doesn't stop if you don't immediately respond to emails or messages. In fact, you might find yourself more productive and engaged with the time you reclaim.

A digital detox doesn't have to be an entire day; it can be as simple as dedicating specific activities or moments to being device-free, such as during meals or while spending time outdoors. If possible, incorporate device-free periods into vacations to fully disconnect and recharge. These practices encourage alternative ways of spending time, leading to more meaningful and fulfilling experiences.

Remote Work Challenges

While remote work offers undeniable advantages—flexibility, reduced commuting time, and the comfort of home—it also comes with unique challenges. To thrive in a remote work environment, individuals must create personalized systems of boundaries, routines, and schedules.

1. Setting Boundaries: Establish clear boundaries between work and personal life. Physical boundaries, like having a dedicated workspace with a door that opens and closes to signal the start and end of your workday, can create structure. Alternatively, implement schedule-based boundaries by starting your day with activities like a workout or meditation and avoiding work emails until designated work hours.

2. Maintaining Routines: Remote work can disrupt daily routines, leading to either overworking or working too little—both of which can result in burnout. Set consistent start and end times for your workday and take regular breaks. Sticking to a structured routine helps prevent your day from unraveling.

3. Combating Isolation: One of the most significant challenges of remote work is the sense of isolation. Relying solely on digital communication may leave you feeling disconnected from your coworkers and the organization as a whole. To counter this, engage in regular video calls, participate in virtual team-building activities, and make an effort to maintain a sense of camaraderie with colleagues.

Conclusion

Technology, when used mindfully, has the power to enhance work-life balance. By setting boundaries, embracing digital detoxes, and addressing the unique challenges of remote work, individuals can reclaim control over their time and foster both personal and professional well-being.

CHAPTER 6

Cultural and Organizational Factors

As workforces become increasingly diverse, the need for research into how work and family dynamics affect different cultural groups has grown significantly. Members of various cultural backgrounds encounter universal human experiences in their work-life balance journeys. However, these experiences are shaped by unique cultural dimensions, making it essential to analyze both their similarities and differences. Understanding these nuances allows us to make credible observations about the diverse work-life balance challenges faced by individuals across the spectrum.

Examining work-life balance through cultural and organizational lenses expands our understanding of the factors at play in a diverse society. While cultural differences are often seen as sources of tension or conflict, they can also become assets that inspire enrichment and creativity. Cultural diversity encompasses differences across a broad range of dimensions, such as ethnicity, race, gender, age, religion, and more. When these differences are embraced in workplaces, they foster opportunities for collaboration, learning, and mutual growth. For many, the workplace is one of the few shared spaces where people from varying cultural backgrounds interact meaningfully, forging friendships and exchanging ideas. This shared experience highlights the potential for diversity to become a wellspring of innovation and enrichment.

Company Policies

While having work-life balance policies in place is a step in the right direction, companies must regularly assess their effectiveness and adapt them to the evolving needs of employees. Polling employees on whether they feel they have a healthy balance, whether their colleagues appear overworked, and how management could offer better support is an excellent starting point. Such feedback helps organizations identify gaps and opportunities for improvement.

Evaluating these policies can be challenging, but tools now exist to measure how a company's practices compare to industry standards. The success of such policies depends largely on a company's overall culture and its commitment to fostering balance among employees. Leaders must take a big-picture approach, recognizing the benefits of supporting work-life balance for both individuals and the organization as a whole.

For managers and business owners, leading by example is paramount. Concrete policies that promote balance—like flexible scheduling, parental leave, or wellness initiatives—demonstrate commitment. Moreover, the behavior of leadership sends a powerful signal. If leaders consistently work late into the night, employees may perceive this as an expectation, undermining the company's work-life balance efforts. By modeling balanced behavior and cultivating an environment of support, leaders can encourage employees to prioritize their well-being.

Societal Norms

Traditional roles and expectations are rapidly evolving, reflecting a broader shift away from outdated societal norms. Fathers today are not just breadwinners—they actively participate in homemaking and parenting responsibilities. Similarly, women are increasingly taking on prominent roles in both the workplace and broader society. These shifts highlight the changing fabric of family dynamics, though they also bring challenges, such as financial pressures and incidents of marital tension tied to shifting norms.

Societal ideals place significant pressure on working parents, burdening them with unrealistic expectations to excel both professionally and personally. Parents are often made to feel inadequate, as societal messages reinforce the myth of the "perfect" mother or father—constantly self-sacrificing, omnipresent for their children, while simultaneously excelling in their careers. This unattainable standard leaves many parents with a lingering sense of "not being good enough."

Breaking free from these myths requires acknowledging and accepting the fluidity of modern family roles. Men are increasingly embracing nontraditional roles, such as stay-at-home parenting, while women are making significant strides in careers traditionally dominated by men. These role reversals demonstrate progress, yet society must continue to challenge the stereotypes and expectations that create unnecessary strain for working families.

Conclusion

Cultural diversity, progressive company policies, and evolving societal norms all play a critical role in shaping work-life balance in modern workplaces. Embracing diversity, fostering inclusive policies, and rejecting unrealistic societal expectations can create an environment where individuals feel supported in achieving harmony between their personal and professional lives.

CHAPTER 7

Work-Life Balance in Different Professions

Work-life balance is an essential consideration across all professions, but its importance and application can vary significantly based on the nature of the work and the personal goals of individuals. Some highly driven professionals may find fulfillment in their work itself and perceive less need for a distinct balance. For such individuals, high motivation and job engagement may take precedence. However, for the majority, work-life balance remains a critical factor in protecting physical and mental health, improving job satisfaction, and maintaining overall quality of life. Respecting and supporting employees' unique definitions of balance through flexible policies and encouragement is key to reducing role conflicts and enhancing workplace harmony.

Context Matters: Variation Across Professions The ease with which work-life balance can be achieved often depends on the demands of the profession. In high-pressure fields like law and medicine, where the work is inherently challenging and intense, achieving balance can feel particularly elusive. Young professionals in these areas, who must learn new skills while handling demanding responsibilities, often struggle to carve out personal time.

By contrast, in professions like bus driving, customer service, or wait staff roles, where the tasks are more predictable and repetitive, work-life balance may be relatively easier to attain. These jobs typically have structured schedules and fewer opportunities for the accumulation of stress associated with job variety or high stakes.

Entrepreneurs and Startups

Entrepreneurs and those in startup environments face a unique set of challenges in achieving work-life balance. Driven by passion and ambition, many business owners and self-employed individuals find it difficult to "switch off" from their work. They may remain accessible 24/7, taking calls at all hours and negotiating deals on weekends or holidays. While this dedication can lead to professional success, it often comes at a personal cost. Time with family and friends, hobbies, leisure, and personal health may be sacrificed in pursuit of business goals.

For self-employed individuals, the lack of formal structures—such as mandated breaks or standard work hours—adds to the challenge. Entrepreneurs must rely on self-discipline and time management to set boundaries and ensure sufficient rest. Without these controls, long hours and continuous work can lead to burnout, both physically and emotionally. However, for those with a strong sense of purpose and motivation, taking intentional breaks and prioritizing personal time can enhance productivity and sustain long-term success.

Healthcare Professionals

Healthcare professionals occupy one of the most demanding fields, requiring immense emotional resilience, compassion, and dedication. Nurses and doctors often deal with life-and-death situations, making stress management a critical skill for their well-being. Social activities with peer groups have proven effective in reducing emotional fatigue, particularly for those working with terminally ill patients. Peer support fosters camaraderie and helps combat feelings of isolation or emotional detachment.

Other essential self-care practices for healthcare workers include ensuring proper sleep, staying hydrated, eating balanced meals, and engaging in regular physical activity to maintain energy and focus. Taking short, meaningful breaks to connect with patients or their families not only fulfills the "Duty of Care" but also brings a sense of purpose and connection back to their work.

Additionally, healthcare professionals benefit from maintaining a mindset of self-compassion. Reminding themselves that "it's not about me" can help separate personal emotions from professional responsibilities. Open communication with colleagues, a sympathetic ear, and careful selection of language in emotionally charged situations are also vital in fostering a supportive and effective care environment.

Conclusion

The nature of work-life balance differs widely across professions, influenced by job demands, individual goals, and workplace structures. High-pressure careers demand deliberate strategies to prevent burnout, while entrepreneurs must practice self-discipline to maintain equilibrium. Healthcare professionals, on the other hand, require a blend of emotional resilience and self-care to balance the unique challenges of their field. Across all professions, cultivating work-life balance is about respecting individual needs and providing the tools, policies, and support necessary to thrive both professionally and personally.

CHAPTER 8

Maintaining Balance Over Time

In this era of lifelong learning, balancing work and life requires continuous adaptation—not only learning new skills for career progression but also understanding how life itself evolves. Forming a sustainable life model depends on staying open to personal growth and engaging with others for insight and inspiration. Joining professional societies, connecting with peers, and learning from those who share your journey can provide invaluable perspective, especially for mothers or women in similar professions. These connections help you build a foundation of shared wisdom and avoid making decisions that might lead to regret.

Life is ever-changing, and staying balanced means periodically reevaluating your values, goals, and progress. Set aside time every 6 to 12 months for self-reflection and planning. Assess what truly matters to you at different stages of life and adjust your strategy as your circumstances and targets shift. If you're balanced today, the key to long-term success lies in proactively redesigning your life as you go. Small, consistent efforts to create happiness and fulfillment can make a lasting difference.

Periodic Assessments

Periodic assessments are a cornerstone of maintaining balance. Taking time every few months—ideally, quarterly—to evaluate your priorities and clarify your roles in both your personal and professional life is essential. Here's how to approach it:

1. **Reflect on Your Priorities:** Ask yourself: What are my current priorities, and how do they align with my career? Consider factors like compensation, creative fulfillment, service to others, parenting responsibilities, and professional credentials. How does my current role stack up against my personal values?
2. **Analyze Practical Demands:** Assess the practical factors influencing your decisions. Do you need to adjust your role within the company, at home, or both? For example:
    - Could flexible working arrangements, like one day of remote work each week, improve balance?
    - Would stepping back temporarily from certain duties help you regain focus?
    - Can the time and effort invested now yield long-term benefits, such as financial security or career growth?
3. **Revisit Your Relationships:** Openly communicate with colleagues, family members, and anyone involved in your life balance. Clarify roles, expectations, and mutual understandings to create a harmonious dynamic. The knowledge gained from these discussions can justify adjustments while respecting everyone's needs.

Periodic assessments aren't easy—they require time, thoughtful contemplation, and a willingness to transform. However, they lead to profound insights that support lasting balance and fulfillment.

Adjusting Priorities

What does balance mean to you? What aspects of your life—your health, relationships, or creative pursuits—require more attention? Adjusting priorities is not just a one-time task but an ongoing process as life evolves.

Historically, work has been essential for survival, shaping our identities and daily routines. Today, with the privilege of choice in many parts of the world, work is less about mere survival and more about meaning. However, without intentional adjustments, we risk being consumed by routines that stifle individuality and personal growth.

Rule No. 1: Set aside dedicated time for your mental, emotional, and physical well-being. Although finding consistent "me" time may seem impossible, achieving balance often requires tough choices—like saying "no" to certain duties, activities, or obligations. Honoring your most pressing needs, values, and desires is a vital first step.

Balance doesn't come easily, but by protecting your personal time and making deliberate changes, you can lead the fulfilling life you deserve. It may mean cutting back on commitments or reshaping your daily patterns, but the investment in your well-being is invaluable.

Conclusion

Maintaining balance over time is a dynamic process. Lifelong learning, periodic assessments, and thoughtful adjustments are integral to creating a life that aligns with your evolving values and goals. By prioritizing your well-being and embracing change, you can achieve lasting harmony between personal fulfillment and professional success.

Conclusion and Future Trends

Work-life balance (WLB) will remain a focal point of societal and organizational discussions in the years to come. While its dimensions may vary across countries due to differing legal, economic, and cultural frameworks, WLB is undoubtedly a defining characteristic of industrialized societies. Despite existing constraints—including structural, societal, and organizational barriers—progress is expected to continue as external pressures drive change at individual, organizational, and societal levels.

Addressing WLB is not a standalone initiative but an integral part of a comprehensive policy package aimed at tackling broad human resource challenges. The ultimate goal is to optimize organizational productivity while enhancing employee well-being. Over time, the scope of WLB has evolved. Once primarily focused on the intersection of work and family life, modern approaches now recognize the importance of supporting the entire lives of employees. This shift is reflected in strategies that encompass diverse aspects of worker well-being, such as flexible leave policies and holistic workplace initiatives.

Looking ahead, achieving sustainable work-life balance will require both employers and policymakers to adopt adaptive, forward-thinking strategies. As societal norms and workplace dynamics continue to evolve, so too must the frameworks that support individuals in managing their professional and personal responsibilities. In this way, WLB remains not only a vital component of individual satisfaction but also a cornerstone of organizational success.

www.ingramcontent.com/pod-product-compliance
Lightning Source LLC
LaVergne TN
LVHW092102060526
838201LV00047B/1525